Caviar
for the
Soul

by

Swan A. Montague, Ph.D.

Published by Swan Fund Pty

Poetry/General-Inspirational

Cover design by Rebekah A. Steele

Poetry/General/Inspirational

ISBN-13:9781503354869

ISBN-10: 1503354865

DEDICATION

To

THE HUMAN RACE

Show us Your Divine countenance
Guide us with new covenants
May we return to the sacred ways
and see the Beloved's eyes in every gaze

CONTENTS

ACKNOWLEDGMENTS

My gratitude is immense for this creative force that continues, ever-surprisingly, to pour through me. It is my life-force, my therapy, my connection to Great Spirit and the Divine as well as the font that nourishes parts of my soul that nothing else reaches. I acknowledge and thank my guides, Yeshua, the Divine Feminine Spirit, (whom I know must have despaired of me as much as I them at times), and the native cultures and spiritual traditions that have uplifted and inspired me during the long, dark nights of no-thing. I have deep, heart-felt gratitude and love for all of those beings in the unseen worlds who reach out their hands and their hearts to us, unknown, invisibly, often thanklessly.

I thank the presence of various muses in my life who catalysed and alchemised this creative force, often by not being there for long – for that I forgive all transgressions as frequently it was those absences that opened this heart and soul to deeper feelings and other worlds.

Grateful recognition to Rebekah Steele who stepped up at the last minute and connected deeply enough to this work to create the beautiful cover image – mermaids, shells, the moon, caviar for my soul, you got it all and I love the finished cover. For the late nights shooting images and colours back and forth and the great spirit of co-creation, thank you, for being you and allowing that creative force to work through you for this and all you do.

My love, gratitude and great appreciation to Dominique Vollaers Simunye, who was my communicator with Great Spirit when I was buried in the tunnel that precedes the unleashing creative force and rebirths its flow. Also Richard Colley, who warmly provided peaceful space, great food, fun and entertainment, whilst I unraveled myself, rested, re-charged and restored, accepted with grace my sensitivities and idiosyncrasies, despite their foreignness to his rational mind – a true gentleman, non-judgmental and kind.

I thank my friends and especially my sons who have been waiting for my creative fire to be expressed and free me up to be with them more, and my youngest who has had to learn infinite patience when the "writer at work' sign goes up and accept the resulting post-labour exhaustion! Thank you, I love you. Your acceptance and allowances have been invaluable and given my soul space to express and stay sane.

I hope the words in these writings will inspire, illuminate, amuse and entertain you and all who read this, especially during times when the curtain comes down, the lights go out, the stage of your life-play goes dark and your soul-table is bare – may you be nourished and blessed by the Spirit that flows through my pen.

AUTHOR'S MESSAGE

These poems, as with everything creative in my life, came to me out of the blue. I can remember when the first poem (in my adult life) really came through in a powerful way, striking me with a sense that something much bigger than me was really happening and very present in my existence. I was writing a flyer for a workshop and contemplating the message I was trying to bring through when it began to write itself in rhyme. The most extraordinary thing about it was that whilst I was writing it, (it was I who was moving my fingers across the keyboard and I who the words were coming through) I was not in control of the keyboard. It had a mind of its own, or it, or I, was taken over by something omnipotent, so all-powerful (and benign) that I could not control it. It just did what it wanted to do with the keyboard. It stuck on capitals, then shifted to lower case spontaneously, skipped or centred lines, it moved where it wanted to and I could not make it do what I thought it should, or tried to make it do.

I did not really realize back then, more than 15 years ago now, the incredible significance of this creative force that was coming into my life. It was from so far outside of me, so much bigger than me, that it is only now, as I write this, that it is fully dawning on me, what this means. It means this creative force, that is available to all those who are called, or maybe chose, is so immense, so massively powerful, that it can come into physical form, through me, through anyone, and literally take over the realm of matter that we are connected to. This is manifestation in its most potent and astonishing form – 'mani' 'fest, to celebrate in the hand, a higher force celebrated through our hands. Neither did I recognize myself as a poet until a specific time in my life. As a child I had won the island eisteddfod where I grew up, out of quite a few entrants, for a poem that I thought was somewhat puerile, but it did rhyme well!

I arrived at a point in my life when I discovered I loved to write, and indeed had been writing The Book of Sahra for some years by the time this recognition of my penchant for verse became clear. As with all my creative outbursts, that book was not something I chose to write, it chose to be written through, and write me. It was an intense labour that literally took over my life for over eleven years, frequently extremely gruelingly, but at times during that mammoth undertaking there was an overtaking of the smaller me and other poems that were not Sahra poured from me.

With Sahra I knew something profound, with extensive implications, was taking place, but with these other poems it was just words, sentiments, insights, deep feelings that had to be expressed. They would light up inside me like a fire, a well wanting to unleash a fountain of intense energy that would perforce burst through and there would be nothing I could do but write, uninterruptedly.

This was more than a creative outlet, it was a life force that exploded within me and rendered life unbearable and impossible until the flow was spent and ink had filled astonishing numbers of pages that became numerous journals in short periods of time.

I did not sleep much; I still do not. As I write this it is 4 a.m. Where I am staying there is a chiming clock whose hours I hear ticking by, chimes denoting another half hour has passed, another hour, or two more. (Clock chimes as I write, it is the dead of night), I cannot sleep – all I can do is write. The creative fire burns in me, through me. The night feels cold, but as I write, the heat builds and I am a perspiring furnace.

What is this force that through me

pours? I find myself in a lull, between phases, aspects and ways of life that are gone, and a new life not yet begun, so I have time to contemplate this force, time and space, finally, to put together these poems that have haunted my nights, and many days, for eons. I re-read them, some for the first or second time only as they come through in such a compulsive virulent flow I just have to keep going with them in the moment, pen flying, there is no time to go back and read.

It was a night such as this when a muse came into my life to whom I am most grateful for the presence and appreciation he showed. He just materialized. We met, somewhere, at a time when my life was very bleak. I had been in Australia for a few years and was very unwell, and, symbiotically, very unhappy.

I had left Santa Fe, New Mexico, very much against my heart's desire or will, a sacrifice I reluctantly made so my son could have his mother and father in the same place at a time when it was important for him and it was clear America was in for a rough ride. I knew this, but it did not assuage my grief at being torn away from the land I loved and that nourished my soul.

When I first had gone to Santa Fe, driven out to that high mountain desert beyond the city, I was moved by a deep and ancient love for the land that was so primordial, my own ancient history was being blasted through every cell of my being, bursting into flower through all my remembering. As the sun set in a deep rosy fire over the late autumn burnished leaves of the cottonwood trees, and the mountains took on their customary plum–coloured haze, the desert floor a molten golden blaze, I abandoned my car on the side of the road, lay down on the ground, face down, and howled. I had come home. Landing in Australia, being driven to my new abode, my heart sank.

Australia felt leaden and grey, the

suburbs dull and mediocre, the rain forest dark, dense and intensely swampy. A pall of misery settled down through me like a wave. "The rainforest is so beautiful," people would say. Yes, I would think, if you like looking at a lot of brown tree-trunks and dense bush between you and the sky. I longed for Santa Fe every day. Even the ocean there did not soothe me, the sea–swan; to the ocean I belong, but I did not love being battered and blown roughly by antipodean winds; they were not the exhilarating wild winds of my beloved Cornish hills, and I hated swimming in the ocean being pounded by pacific (nothing peaceful about them) waves. Further more my heart was soon very badly broken.

When the muse and I met, my broken heart had led me to double pneumonia, a collapsed lung and Ross River Fever. I crawled around for months, dragging myself through the day, showing up only for my son. When my son was not with me, my only companions were pen and notebook. Moving, breathing, living was excruciating, writing the only relief. I wrote some of the most profound chapters of Sahra from the daybed on which I lived.

I remember not where or how the muse and I met, however we swapped phone numbers and talked about meeting up again, but that was not to be our fate. My mobile phone was my only connection to the world and I would often send texts during my sleepless nights, Out of the blue he was there too, another midnight mystical wanderer. He loved poetry and we would read and quote poems to each other through the late hours from the first midnight phone call, which ended as the depth of the night sky turned to dawn.

One night, after many such nocturnal meanderings through the worlds of poets, I summoned enough bravado to read one of my own poems. I found my voice, reading a quite long poem that had never been read aloud before. None of them had. I had not read them, or showed them to any, and I had not heard them.

I heard it through his soul that night. When I came to the end I could feel him taking the poem in. The long silence that ensued was a hiatus of seemingly immense, nervous portent. He drew in a long, slow, deep breath, equally slowly exhaling, and there was another silence before he spoke. He had the most beautiful deep rich voice, like velvet, with which I was quite in love, and was very au-fait with poetry and literature.

"Who was that?" he asked. I had not told him I was going to read one of my own poems, or even that I wrote poems. I did not consider myself a poet. I didn't speak; I could not. "It's so familiar, yet I can't place it," he continued. "Byron?" he asked. I was in shock. Byron? Could he possibly think that Byron wrote my words, how could this be? He continued, "No, not Byron, maybe Shakespeare. Not really, I don't recognise it, but it's like Byron or Shakespeare combined." He went on to list an array of famous poets. I was astonished and bemused. Still to this day I am amazed. He was the perfect muse, he inspired and admired. He was not in my life long, and I was sad when he went away. He was the man I remembered and wrote the poem about in 'The Garden of Adam and Eve'. We only met twice briefly in person, meeting in a powerful way, but the gift was given, destiny had brought to me the reality I needed to see, that maybe not just for me these poems had meaning.

As I write this, another night gone by, my Apple and I, I am so grateful for the few muses and friends who, over time, have come into my life, who never stayed long, but their gifts were given, their job was done. They have inspired, encouraged, seen, felt and motivated; their belief, always astounding to me, has fuelled this fire that continues to burn through me. I put together these poems now in the hope that they, in some profound or gentle way, touch each one of you.

Some are good, occasionally sassy, others a little corny maybe, but all are heart-felt, deep experiences and ancient memories, higher knowing, that come from somewhere within and without, that is me and yet something greater than me, that insists on being expressed, voiced, night or day, whatever may be. I hope that they will be part of this new world awakening that is taking place. They are the voice of the Divine Feminine that is being birthed everywhere, in every way, that is leading the way forward now, and must be heard and have its say. I hope these poems will uplift and inspire, make you laugh, make you cry, whatever sentiments are unleashed, that you will find something in here to take you deeper, take you higher.

May the creative force be with me,

and you, always, and now and then can I please get some sleep!

With lovelight blessings,
Swan

AUTHOR'S NOTE

When I speak of God, Jesus, Goddess, I am not referring to any religious or ecumenical hierarchy or dogma. I can neither praise any religion that is based on a separatist culture of God, the masculine, religious or class hierarchy, nor any canon, creed or precept that believes any God is better or more important than another's. I believe in the God/Goddess within. I love and revere the mystical teacher/healer, Yeshua (Jesus), who established no church, wrote down no laws or sermons, but taught the true meaning of love, and life.

My personal favourite of the many spiritual cultures and traditions is the Indian Nations of the Americas. I believe, and teach, the Spirit of Oneness, Divine Love, also known as Source, Creator, Great Spirit, Great Mystery, the Beloved, God, Goddess, Earth Mother, Mother nature, the Universe ~ a life-force that exists within each one of us, recognised or unacknowledged, that is far greater than anything we can imagine yet we are each unique facets of, that is everyone's inherent birthright and that is our true highest, most glorious and most powerful all-knowing Self.

For aeons, as far back as the written word reaches and beyond, into the ancient teachings of races who passed their spiritual culture down through generations with spoken and written word as well as symbols, re-incarnation has been their inherent fundamental tenet, the basis of all such spiritual cultures and the foundation for all their understanding, teachings and fruitful, more harmonious ways of living – the cornerstone of the meaning of life.

It was removed from the bible during the Nicaean Council of A.D.325 in an act I consider indubitably the greatest ever dis-service to humanity. How can life possibly be a random, arbitrary, luck of the draw, one-time, one shot, one take, temporary existence – what sense does that make? Who then decides who gets a great life or a life of struggle? Without an understanding and the intrinsic experience or acceptance of the infinite spirit and the eternal soul, remembering who we have been and all we are, as well as the potential to evolve into all we can be, life has little meaning. A finite life, with such limited potential for spiritual and human evolution is a massive misconstruction that could be humanity's greatest, and possibly most serious demise. If we do not know this about ourselves: who and all we are have been and can be, then how can we choose to be who we want to be or be the best we can be? And what would be the point?

1

GOD'S BREATH

We are infinite love,
without it bereft
eternal death
spiraling cycle of rebirth
Life's play of tears and mirth
We are God's breath

2

THE CALL OF LOVE

Why run from love,
why not meet it face to face?
Is it not a gift from above,
a blessing of immense grace?

If love you are not willing to meet,
if Goddess and yourself you would cheat,
the God within not turn to greet,
then Maya* you will endlessly repeat

To face true love you have to be brave
stake your claim and plant your stave
stop hiding in your safe cave
A path to love with your heart's blood
 pave

Love is the light of human lives,
the only way to end the strife.
Take love home and make her your wife
For love only, toil and strive

Love is the way the truth and the light
Of this one thing only never lose sight
If the walls of your heart are blocked and
 tight
then fear more loss and fear will incite

So wear your love and bear your all
Strip yourself naked, and stand tall
If you always chose love you cannot fall
Only then are you invited to the divine
 ball

In true love there can be no mistake.
What will it take
for this treatise in you to awake,
that you can swim in an everlasting love-
 lake?

Love bursts open every locked window
 and door
It busts you right to the floor
until you know you can take no more
and allow yourself, in fullness, to adore

Love is heaven's most priceless gift
t'will heal all wounds when it opens rifts
Let yourself on the sea of love drift
and into heaven you will soon lift

There really is no other way
ere you continue your struggle endless
 days
When the sun of love shines, make hay
Though it will knock you for six, for
 divine love pray

Drop all defences, naked on the ground
 lay
Open your arms and open stay
Bare your soul and to the moon bray
The sun and the stars will show you the
 way

So when love knocks loudly at your door
drop all defenses to the floor
Surrender knowing there is no more
than to answer love's call and fully adore

*Maya ~ illusion

3

THROB

I can love you now
even when you are not there for me
I can love you when you are not here
with me
I am love

I can love you always when
revisiting eternity now and then
I know this love will always call you back
to me,
as surely as I know the leaves will once
more bedeck the trees
and the flowers again dance in the breeze.
If they don't
then we are really lost
and the universe will throb
with one last sob.

4

NO FEAR

When you are near
there is nothing to fear
Light kisses away tears
when pain through heart sears
Looking into your eye (I),
Knowing love is no lie
Releasing deep soul sigh
as tears on lips dry
Feeling your arms
Touching silk balm
Weaving words of love with magical yarn
Wrapping in angel's hair
Raging storms are calmed

Soul singing in your softness
Skin ringing to your caress
Spirit humming to your embrace
Blood drumming in passionate interlace
Heart melting hearing your voice
Essence merging with yours

Even Heavenly Father must rejoice
at this, the love of all folklores

To be with you forever
to leave your side never
Nothing would I fear
When You are near.

5

TOUCH YOU UPON A STAR

There you are
I felt I could reach out and touch you
 upon a star
Distance otherwise perfect stillness of
starry night mars.
Loving you from afar

Bed cold and friendless
Night without you is endless
Starry remembrance of bliss
And nights of sweet tenderness.

Oh to see you my friend!
When will me meet again?
Be it this life or next
I am holding my breath

Spiraling cycles of time
Wrap themselves around me like vines
The sip of your wine
lingers forever in heart's mind.

Dawn is once more here
Amber light that shadows fear
As awakening world appears
Dew drops form unshed tears

These waters run deep
Cannot even weep
It's too late to sleep
As back into the night the shadows of my
 dreams creep

The stars are gone
but I will search for you in the sun
Me thinks the searching will never be
 done
for You are the only one.

I will reach for you in the stars
I will seek you wherever you are
I will be with you always however far
Nothing can ever this love mar.

6

ULTIMATE DHARMA

I'm doing my best to stay off the edge
when between the divine and mine soul
  looms an invisible hedge
There's a hundred and fifty foot precipice
  and I'm on the ledge
Can it be so far up the mountain and still
  so much mud to dredge?

It's so scary to be so out of control
Slipping and sliding in a long downhill
  roll
I no longer know who I am and I've lost
  my soul
This ego needs keeping under twenty-
  four-hour patrol

What a to do to be without you, or You,
Spirit sinks into the depths of the blue
Emotions over-cooked in a curried stew
Light and energy bodies a motley crew

If only I could stop chasing my tail
or banging my head on this metal rail
Do my nerves constantly have to be
  assailed
by memories of all we have tried, tested
  and failed?

Is there anything more I can or need to
  do?
How long do I have to be enslaved to
  ego's confining curfew?
Surely it's time salvation be due,
have I not suffered long enough with this
  separation from You

Please come to me now love divine
I long to drink of your blood red wine
For divine ecstasy to be forever mine
I would die over and over and live only
  for this love sublime

To know 'twas always and always will be
  mine
A love that would last till the end of time

A love with no betrayal nor bind
Yet of this love right now there is no sign

Is it really true that it's out there
  somewhere?
Pray tell is it in here, or over there?
and how do I know if it be true or the
  devil's lair
Please bring me mon mari, père, fils, et
  frère

And in him, above all, my best friend
that we may love each other until the end
And I will allow my heart to be wide-
  open rent
to receive such a blessing and Godsend

So please God send me this all
May this please be my last fall?
Catch me before I hit the wall
Restart my heart for it has stalled

Please give me an injection to kick-start
 my heart
An intravenous love drug from which
 never to be parted
A tantric infusion of love prana*
Divine Union, the ultimate Dharma**

*Prana ~ life-force

**Dharma The word "dharma" comes from the
Sanskrit root dhri, meaning to uphold or to sustain,
that which upholds or sustains the positive order of
things: the nation, the community, the family and
ultimately even the universe."

7

THE ONLY SOLUTION

Pure Devotion
Soul the Lotion
Slow the Motion
Physical Emotion
Spread the Notion
Time is an Illusion
Spirit is the Fusion
Higher Love the Potion

8

EYES OF TOASTED HONEY

Eyes of toasted honey that gleam
From the heart remembered sweetness
  beams
Who we are now is not as it seems
Ancient lovelight connection through
  our veins streams

Mystical moment of acquainting anew
I opened my heart and to the core of me
  you flew
Strong and deep these memories of you
On this love there can be no curfew

Blue.... I thought those eyes from afar
But no, tinged with green and filled with
  stars.
Filled with stars, yay they are
Yet bathed in toasted honey, they are
  beyond par

How divine is your open heart
Feeling you mine eyes smart
To be close to you is to fear being apart.
Only the stars know what course this
 love will chart

Eyes of toasted honey
I would have thee feast on me
Make me your vessel and sail me across
 the sea
Fly with me on a mystical love journey

Sing to me as you play your oud
Make this love your daily food
In love's full essence let us be imbued
Out of the cross I bear may a divine heart
 thus be hued.

9

COME TO ME SOON

Divine lover, come to me soon
Come to me for the Aquarian full moon
that my juices may flow to the sound of
 your croon
Come, let us bathe in the sound of divine
 lovelight tunes

10

CHARIOT OF LIGHT

I saw a vision of you last night
You streamed towards me in a chariot of
 golden light
Then came a message from you
and I knew my vision was true

Who are you,
Sun bursting out of the blue?
Clothed in Apollo's shining rays
burning with the fire of Gods you blaze

For you there can be no compromise
The all-seeing light is in your eyes
A god's heart in you does arise
and the love of a goddess must be your
 prize.

11

ALWAYS AND FOREVER

And so, divine love,
please be my lover
In love from head to toe
do me cover
Love me wide open tonight,
Now, always and forever

FIRE OF GRACE

The fire of Grace
is to die in love's embrace,
burn in hell's furnace
as the knife cuts away the mask that
  hides love's True Face

Heart that loves without breaking is a
  fragile shell
Divine loves' blessings amazing and
  terrible,
Love cooks to perfection in the fires of
  hell,
Hides in the water at bottom of well

Divine Love is first worn as a crown
but sooner or later it must filter down
Its voice washing right through you is
  the primordial sound
Open to it or in it be drowned

Love is the road, and all roads lead to
 Rome
where, grounding, love's knife finally
 comes home
Love's knife, razor sharp, slices the lover,
 its stone,
as you sing the Universal word – Aum*

On broken wings of love fly even higher
Lotuses flower in the heart's mire
Divine Soul roasts in Grace's Fire
Divine Heart forged on love's pyre

In the fire of grace wildly dance
In the Fire of Grace, only love stands a
 chance
Blindly whirl in the mystic's trance
As out of chaos, balance is enhanced

Let the Fire of Grace through you swirl
Souls, round and round like dervishes,
 twirl

So splatter love from your skirts as you
 whirl
that love may fly unfettered on wings
 unfurled

Surrender your heart to the Fire of
 Grace
Surrender your mind to love's embrace
Let go, give up, lose all trace
of all that masks the beloved's True Face

*Aum ~ Om (also spelled **Aum**) Hindu sacred
sound that is considered the greatest of all mantras,
comprising three worlds – earth, atmosphere, and
heaven, three major Hindu gods – Brahma, Vishnu,
and Siva, three sacred Vedic scriptures – Rg, Yajur,
and Sama. Om mystically embodies the **essence of
the entire universe**. And a philosophical belief
that God first created sound and the universe arose
from it. A most sacred sound, Om is the root of the
universe, everything that exists and continues to
hold everything together.

DARK NIGHTS

Dark night of the soul...
Hello hole!
Cannot control where or when
You just have to go there again,
 and again.

When the divine shines its light
It may be day or night
Control it you cannot do
But you'll surely know when it happens
 to you.

When that bell tolls
be aware all souls.
Look for the gold
with eyes blindfold

Only one way out
through fear and doubt,
gaping chasms
monsters and miasms

Then you find
the light divine
behind shadows shines.
T'was always thine

For how long were you lost
Wandering in the forest?
Or on stormy seas tossed
chasing what quest.

Did you fall little angels?
Did you choose earth's schools?
Did you not know your cup was full
or was to know yourself a greater pull?

Where to go from here?
Back through the fear
When your heart floods with tears
Love is near.

PRAYER
FOR
DARK NIGHTS

May you find
The light divine
That behind shadows shines
Remember, 'tis always thine

14

HURT, BY HUMANS

Searching the labyrinths of the mind
for some grain of truth to find
The hurts of humankind

Searching, searching, everywhere
For beings who are really there,
Giving nothing, just showing they care

Lost and lonely roads to roam,
so sad and all alone
Return to God, go home, go home

But we are all Gods, the empty cry
Too much fear, fear to die –
the ultimate human lie

The self, the Self, is all that exists
wandering blindly through the mists
falling into soul's abyss

By love, and love alone, we are buoyed
as we sink into the void
Love is all there is, by all to be enjoyed

Yes, love is God, and God is always
 there,
but humans need human care
their pain and sorrow in love to share

A human soul that says "I know,
I'm here for you, I don't have to go
I feel you, in the underworld way below"

Down, down, down in the dark
longing for the light, the spark,
I'm here, I'm here, wish falls, a silent hark

The longing for a hand, an arm,
held in embrace, restored to calm
Love, love, love ~ Love to embalm

A little ray of hope, of light
not yet strong, not yet bright,
filtering through the veil of night

Until the end, until humans grow
   in love and light, until they know they
            are one with God's glow,
there is nowhere else to go

15

THE RED ROAD

Let me walk once more the red road
Raise my spirit and lighten my load
Let me gaze upon your Divine Face
Bless and forgive this human race

Teach us to create anew
For too long we have been blind to all we
 do
Heal the pattern of human tragedy
Deliver us from the darkness of our
 travesties

Let us bathe in the calm waters of the
 Mother
May men greet each other as brothers
For You are the wise mighty all-
 powerful Father
and the Mother that rebirths us into the
 eternal hereafter

Show us Your Divine countenance
Guide us with new covenants
May we return to the sacred ways
and see the Beloved's eyes in every gaze

16

TO GAUL

Words have I found, now I must raise my
 voice
Travesties everywhere abound, I have no
 choice
To France I am bound,
before in this dearth I am drowned

To Avignon I hear the call
Antipodean life for me does pall
"Ere my soul into fatal ennui falls
I pack up my life and head to Gaul

Towering walls of magnificent history
I flee to the land of fragrant beauty,
 fertility
where earth dances to ancient magic and
 mystery
and romantic love touches the soul and
 sets it free

The Sacred World Renaissance is my
  guild,
Temple arts I go to build,
spiritual culture that the hearts of simple
  man will fill
I follow my soul's calling and Divine
  Mother's will

When the first almond buds are birthed
  by the trees
and the perfume of lavender floats on the
  breeze
dancing through the plane trees' first
  proffering of huge leaves
I will be packed, ready to leave, complete

With wisteria clothed in cascading
  blooms
nightingale singing to spring full moon
Life and love I will create anew
as to the past I say adieu

In this dream come and take part
of divine music and sacred arts
To this divine reunion I call my divine
 consort
and all who in divine love wish creatively
 to cavort

T'is time to fill our lives with light divine
To reunite the Divine spirit–lines,
all who in divine love wish to recline
and imbibe from the true grail of Christic
 wine

Let us converge in this resting place
and freely abound in God's blessed grace
where once people fled religious
 sacrilege's blaze
May we birth and to a new divine era
 give praise

17

FIELD OF DREAMS

Come with me to my field of dreams
in a world where exist no seams
Love and truth pour forth in rhymes and
 reams.
All is exactly as should be.

T'is a field of love in which I wander
Doves coo songs fonder
On this sea of feeling bonded,
sail with me over yonder
Love growing blissfully stronger
uniting in a love of absolute wonder,
Gazing, feeling, breathing deeper, longer

Heart reels
Soul feels
Gentle laughter peels
Love knows no seal

Angels dancing up above.
Swathing hearts in infinite love
Touching tenderly with kid glove
I would brush your cheek with the wings
  of a dove

Come with me to my field of dreams
Dance with me in the light of silver
  moonbeams
While liquid light of love streams
Bask naked as morning sun on lovers
  gleams

Divine trance
Flowers dance
Unicorns once again prance
Love enhanced

In the heavenly light of the lovers'
  domain
only feelings of bliss remain

Nothing to lose, nothing to gain
just eyes of love reflecting love's refrain.

Ecstatic love for all to see
Paradise vibrantly living truth and
 beauty.
If your heart be true, wild and free
wander in this field of dreams with me

Nature's might
Auras alight
Joy so bright
Love is right

18

GODDESS' CREAM

You came to me in a velvet dream
Dipped your fingers in goddess cream
Oh, what divine light streamed!
Bright as nebula we beamed

In my dreams you will return
In flames of divine union will we burn
Shades of love-filled groans
Passion's desire in deep tones

Love's enflamed voice
Souls rejoice
Explosions of light
when souls reunite

Heavenly light of love, all-seeing Entire
being divine light streaming
Human bonds dissolving, freeing
Love dissolution, the ultimate freeing

To lay awake until day break
drifting dreamily our blissful love-lake
or to slumber at my dreams to wonder,
are you real or did I you conjure?

Will you stay with me, in love to
  wander?
Let us not such reflection squander
Unite with me in celestial gondola
our love flowing ever stronger

For 'tis a new world we create
in which only true love can satiate
Resolving forever fear and hate
Food of love for all on golden plates

Souls blessed come to no harm
E'en they die in love's arms
To die to love in such balm
is divine love musk, angels' psalms.

So come again soon
to love by the light of the moon,
soaring to me through the stars
    Oh, what heavenly love legacy is ours!

19

JUST LIGHT

It's light, just light,
No light without love.
More light, more love.
The light burns,
burns bright,
within and above,
goes deep,
too deep even to weep,
or eat,
or sleep.

Open only to love,
more love,
receiving it from above,
deep within
knowing all it is, is love,
only love,
the ending and beginning

Touched, kid glove.
Heart ripped open,

ego's last reserves broken,
revealing what has so long
been fought to preserve,
that true love
I, you, we,
really deserve

The truth can no longer be swerved.
When exactly did humanity lose its
 nerve?
What on earth happened to verve?
Jesus, ace after ace, you serve!

Shall we cower at the line and pretend
we don't see
that truth doeth not bend
and You love he, she, me.

Why does it burn,
this, that the heart does so yearn?
The lie, the lie, the lie –
I cannot be worthy, oh no, not I!

For eons since You left this lie
has become a global outcry.

So many for so little love vie.
Nothing left to do but let angel wings
soar and fly

For this, to all else now we must
 surrender and die –
to know that everyone is loved as I
That I am loved is for me to know
That all are loved is for each one of us to
 show
The seeds of this love I now sow
as I weave the heavenly tableau
This is the celestial cry – AHO!

Let this love wash away all tears
May there be no more need for fear
Heaven is near
when You are here

So feel this love deep within
It heals all that is without (sin)
With You now, let this journey begin
Let it in
                    Aho, Amen.

20

LIFE PASSING BY

Sometimes you stop and see life passing
 by
You become the witness and wonder why
Failing to understand the mystery, you
 sigh,
Did I come here to live, birth and die?

What did I really come here to do,
who am I and who are you?
All the things we do, we do for who,
and am I one of the masses, or one of the
 few?

Does it really matter if it doesn't make
 sense?
Are you happy to spend your life sitting
 on a fence?
Death cares not if you're intelligent or
 dense
What counts is making a
 difference

Laughing at the nonsensity
Choosing fame or anonymity
Caught up in absurdity
All counts for nothing with no
 authenticity

We sleep and we wake
We cook and we bake
We climb the highest mountains,
  meditate on lakes
We love and we hate, we give and we
 take

We experience life and we spiral around
thoughts and feelings continuously
 abound
Paradise lost, paradise found
Ever evolving meaning and theory we
 expound

Important only to be reverential
Humanitarian, not bestial
It's really all existential
Remembering our essence, pure, celestial

One thing is for sure, life continues to
 pass,
Only as long as destiny does anything
 last.
Holding on becomes a farce
though letting go can leave us aghast

At the end of life there is one truth left
We are all bereaved, without God bereft,
Loss of the divine is a terrible theft
Knowing ourselves to be divine is to be
 blessed

Whether we stay at home or travel afar
what is important is to know who we are
We are guided by planets and inspired
 by stars
The only way forward is to keep opening
 our hearts

Loves will come and deaths will go
Births overcome, our children grow

We hope to see the flowers of the seeds
we sow
and love it best in a harmonious flow
But when times are hard we grow the
 most,
though we find ourselves staggering from
 post to post
Of success it's dangerous to boast
Fruits of the ego haunt us like ghosts

Sometimes the signposts are hard to find
Which way next, where are the signs?
Life's passing by and we're running out
 of time
It's too difficult a dance or a mysterious
 mime

One way or another at times it's hard
joyful moments can easily be marred
We study the planets and we read the
 cards
spirit gets burnt, souls charred

The scars are the outlines of self-
    portraits,
gifts and creations our own unique arts
Whether it be a constant surprise of pre-
    ordained fate
your story can be read in the walls of
    your heart

So as life passes by, what should we do
but let our own unique, diamond light
    shine through
Through the thick and the thin, the pink
    and the blue
the greatest truth is
        that You are loved and Love is you

21

INK

My lungs are full of black ink
they're so painful it's hard to think
Naught for me to do but sink
let emotions flow to the brink
Pour forth my story in one of this
planet's greatest gifts – ink!

Imagine a world without ink, if you
 please,
the genius of Coleridge, Byron,
 Shakespeare, Hafiz,
Rumi, Dante, so many others, into
 oblivion to sink.
The past would be gone in a blink.

Pen kisses paper and words bow to
 thoughts
Meaning birthed from feelings,
 given life, caught,

Understanding, long sought.
layers of hidden truths, unpeeling

These words penned
are feelings' end
What a divine creation, this art,
to give life to the Christ-Heart.

22

JOSS

*This poem I wrote as a lament to my son who
was taken from me, a long time ago, at seven
years old, that he might know.........
I dedicate this to mothers and fathers all over
the world who live with the loss of their beloved
children. May your hearts be healed and come
to know that life is eternal and our children
come back to us when we let them go!*

My dear Joss
What a loss!
On my heart is embossed
the price that losing you has cost!

If I do not write
it is not out of spite.
It does not feel right
to share with you my heart's plight

I love you so
'though I guess you don't know.

Oft my tears flow
that I have not seen you grow

How fares your heart
when for so long we have been apart?
Navigating emotion's oceans with no
 chart,
separation is a painful art

How do you really feel?
Do you wonder if your mother was ever
 real?
A mother's love you cannot steal
without leaving a wound hard to heal

I cry for the toll
I wonder for your soul
In your heart, too, is there a hole
for the mother's love that from you was
 stole?

It was not my wish to be so far away
I tried everything this distance to allay
Then it was too painful to stay,
too harrowing and tragic a play

When from you I never heard
No sign, no message, no reply, no word
It seemed in you for me no feeling was
 stirred
That it was easier for you without me,
 'though it seems absurd.

My darling, you I never wanted to leave
Do you feel as I, sad and bereaved?
Does your heart relentlessly grieve?
I have loved you always, this you must
 believe.

I pray one day there will be reprieve
that our lives will again together weave
You will come home and never for long
 leave
to your new brother and I you will once
 more cleave

So, my darling, I trust you are well,
that we will meet again soon and of your
 life you will tell,
We will pick up again from where we fell
 and once again ring celebration's bell.

In love we will reunite
Ancient history will obliterate our plight
That one day you will know true light
that for love of you I gave up the fight.

It was for you that I let go
rather than drag you through wind, hail
 and snow
The truth of the lies was too painful for
 you to know.
I could find no way without hurting you
 the truth to show.

Back then you did not want to see
What you were being told was not real
I always loved and was committed to thee
Your father simply would not let it be

Of his love for you I am sure
'though his methods I have abhorred
His soul was lost, as mine, but his spirit
 was poor.
'Though he went to church, t'was ever I
 who knocked on God's door

Your father from the truth hid
His bitter feelings he kept under lid
Many evil deeds he did
For your soul he plotted and secretly bid

For love of you, years I have been silent
heart and soul sorely rent
The truth can no longer be burned or
 bent
The energy to hold this inside has all
 been spent

In my heart lives a place for you
Sometimes I cry, think of you, and rue
I wonder how you do
and if you wonder how I am too

I love you anyway
I hold the thought of you coming one
 day,
of how much we will have to say
and imagine we will laugh, sing and play

Do you remember singing the song "You
  gotta be bold,
You gotta be bad, you gotta be wiser"?
The story will be told as in my arms I will
  you enfold
And we'll play it again and sing even
  louder

Our tears we will dry
with great sighs
We will heal the lies
as in joyful lasting reunion we will arise

And so it is
And so it shall be
In the name of Divine Love
By Divine Decree!

23

HO SWEET SORROW

Ho, sweet Sorrow,
old friend,
I feel you yet again
Heart held in icy hand
crushing life as foot on sand
Weeping soul
dying in love's black hole

When love lies,
runs to the arms of fear,
denies, hides, denies
bleeding heart, mortally speared, cries
where is my old friend, Love?
You have always been my friend
Will you be there at the end?

STAY WITH ME

Stay with me tonight
lay your head upon my pillow
Dance with me under the moonlight
Let my cares drift away knowing
 everything's allright

Love me tonight
Hold me close, don't let me take fright
Run your fingers through my hair
Soothe away my cares

Spirit come into me
make love to the very core of me
so deep to the depth of me
I feel you right to the heart of me

I beg you to now come unto me
I need you to not feel the pain in me
You are the only way to release me
Come, set me free

Spirit, do not fly away and leave me
Do not leave me here in this world
 without thee
Whatever you do, never bereave me
Without you I am lost to me

Without you it's hell, such a sad place
  to be
the grief goes on forever, don't you see?
Infinite death way down deep in me
Without full union of love with thee

Oh Lord raise me up to Thee
That I may marvel at all You feel and see
I will let you forever in my heart be
Then I will be peaceful, bountiful and
 free

PRAYER
STAY WITH ME

Beloved Divine
Oh Lord raise your people up to thee
That they may marvel at all you feel
 and see
May You forever in all hearts be
That human souls be bountiful, peaceful
 and free

25

SEASON DANCES,
JOURNEYS OF THE HEART

Of the journey of the heart,
you will wonder when did it start,
how long will it last
and one day will we part?

Heart–beat keeps missing –
Love ascending
Do we dance forever in bliss
at divine love's wedding?

Loving all night
Holding so tight
Merging with such might
Deepening, connecting sight

Lilac trees in the wind bending
Branches reaching into each other, hearts
 extending

May it be never–ending,
never descending

This wind that blows away old memories
 with the leaves,
like lovers, every moment seizes
In this love we can only fiercely believe
fire enough to melt winter freeze

Like season dances
two thousand naked stances
this love advances
deepening as it prances

It rises like the morning sun
but lingers ere the day is done
Flies through night skies
 where chelas run
Bursts into fragrant flowered branches
 with amaranth wisteria overhung

Seeds of passion germinating way
 down low,
deepening, still as white winter snow

Love's breath like snowflakes melts in the hand
painting a magical new land

With the wings of the butterflies it flutters
 in spring,
To the song of the bird, love's heart sings.
like almond blossoms, bursts open, flowering,
mirroring the rhythm of butterfly's joyfully
 quivering wings.

Then the heat of summer sun's rays
surges in smoky passion's fiery haze
Blissful union, held in heated gaze
Infinite love mirrored in the mirage blaze

Veils float away as autumn leaves fall
like hearts dancing as trees in the breeze
 of love stand tall
Burnished tones of love enthrall
Angel of love enfolding lovers in
 feathered shawl

The journey of the heart never ends
From one season to the next it bends

Weathered and seasoned, only deepening
It has its own rhyme and knows no reason

Around, around, around and around,
through cycles of time it abounds
Its sigh is the primordial sound
of lovers' rapture in the bliss they are bound

As the season dances
through love's various trances
The heart, like the deer prances,
marveling in love's infinite stances

26

THE CALL OF LOVE

Why run from love,
why not meet it face to face?
Is it not a gift from above,
a blessing of immense grace?

If love you are not willing to meet,
If Goddess and yourself you would cheat
the God within not turn to greet,
then Maya* you will endlessly repeat

To face true love you have to be brave
Stake your claim and plant your stave,
Stop hiding in a safe cave
A path to love with your heart's blood
   must be paved

Love is the light of human lives,
the only way to end the strife.
Take love home and make her your wife
For love only, toil and strive

Love is the way the truth and the light
Of this one thing only never lose sight
If the walls of your heart are blocked and
 tight
then fear more loss and fear incites

So wear your love and bear your all
Strip yourself naked, and stand tall
If you chose always love you cannot fall
Only then are you invited to the divine
 ball

In true love there can be no mistake.
What will it take
for this treatise in you to awake?
You can swim in an everlasting love-lake

Love bursts open every locked window
 and door
It busts you right to the floor
until you know you can take no more
and allow yourself, in fullness, to adore

Love is heaven's most priceless gift
t'will heal all wounds when it opens the
 rifts
Let yourself on the sea of love drift
and into heaven you will soon lift

There really is no other way
ere you continue your struggle endless
 days
When the sun of love shines, make hay
Though it will knock you for six, for
 divine love pray

Drop your defenses, naked on the
 ground lay
Open your arms and open stay
Bare your soul and to the moon bray
The sun and the stars will show you the
 way

So when love knocks loudly at your door
drop all defenses to the floor

Surrender knowing there is no more
than to answer love's call and fully adore.

*Maya – (Sanskrit) Illusion

27

WE ARE ONE

We are one
no separation.
You are here –
such elation

We are one
the past is done
fear cessation
perfect creation

We are one
we sing the same song
No limitation
Love initiations

We are one
melting stone
love potion
in exquisite motion

We are one
apart for too long
seething emotion
utter devotion

We are one
Separation done
New life has begun
Within us, earth moon stars and sun

IN-FORMED

*Dedicated to my friend, healer Ian Cambell, a
friend and healer to the rescue, who referred
to family drama as being in-formed. .
With love and gratitude to you, Ian*

In-formed
from the moment born
To certain conditions forsworn

Into earthly illusion delved
Lost remembering of true self
higher power bereft on celestial shelf

Intense labour to re-form
dying to the lie, being reborn
learning the falsity to spawn

Gradually remembering who we are
unique aspect of the Divine, without par
knowing from Heaven
we can never be barred

ESSENCE

Through sacred veils
divine soul hails

Many lives many tales
spirit vessel sails.

Remember who you are
Essence extending afar.

RETURN TO THE GARDEN OF ADAM AND EVE (PAST LIFE)

I saw a past life
when I was your wife
Over me stood a man with a knife

Behind me cowered our daughter
Our whole tribe faced threat of slaughter
We both knew you would do what you
 ought to

We looked long and deep into each
 other's eyes
Both knowing no escape from this fatal
 demise
That you would have to make the
 ultimate sacrifice

I knew what you would have to do
Abject dread between us grew
Momentarily I closed my eyes, signaling
 good–bye to you

I watched you close your eyes, resigned,
When you opened them again with grief
 were they blind
Unable to watch, you walked away as
  knife struck me from behind

I knew you had no choice but,
  abandoning, to betray
Yet as I died my heart sank in dismay
though it was clear there really was no
 other way

The other men of the village, gone away
Many of the tribe old and grey
Women and children pure, innocent and
gay

What happened to our daughter I never
 knew

I already knew what next you would do
when the slaughterers left having taken
 their due

As your world turned black
you stood in silence and turned your
 back
You walked away and never looked back

Stoic and stalwart but filled with grief
without a word you took your leave
to bereave yourself as you had been
 bereaved

The tears of this parting flow on
Though the bodies that lived it are long
 gone
Fears are that this love will remain
 undone

From that abyss we have returned
Through so many fires we have been
 burned
Lessons of love's losses have we learned

So come to me now, please
Let us every moment seize
Wont you return with me to the garden
of Adam and Eve?

31

LOVING EFFORTLESSLY

Does love always end in tragedy?
Is romance tragedy or tragedy romance?
Is life a divine comedy and love its
 prodigy
or does it go on forever in an endless
 dance?

Will I see you again,
in this life or next?
Do we restart where we began,
and when it ends will I be so perplexed?

If you leave me now, will I leave you next
 time?
Will it be you who tries to make heartbreak rhyme
And I who behind the veils hides while
 others suffer at love you deride?

So what of this parody,
is soul enhanced by fortune and chance?
Ecstatically or wretchedly,
when it comes round again, how will we
   dance?

What hope of loving endlessly, of living
   happily?
What about righ now, not next life,
an end right now to heartbreak and strife
Loving effortlessly.

32

FIRE WHEEL

Fire wheel turns
Sun cycle Rotation
Lessons learned
One earth, one nation

33

THE MATERIAL WAR ~ LOOK TO THE SUN

Don't let the material war get you down.
Keep looking into the Sun.
Keep looking to the Son.
Full feeling attention on heart,
keep eyes on Sun, Son,
This is the only way forward.

Sun, Daughter
Daughter, Son,
Mother, Lover
You are all one.
"Tis not a personal war
"Tis a material one,
"Tis not the war of the Father
Nor of His Son.
It is the cycle of the Universe
and a new one has already begun

So, die, Old, and grow Young,
the Spirit in you has always won.
Peace hath the Soul
that from the Devil does not run.
("I will not strike back and I will not turn
 aside,"
said Gandhi, and from the devil he did
 not hide.)
As above, so below,
solar storms ebb and flow.
There is nowhere in the Universe
Sun's bio-electromagnetic field will not
 go.
Spirit is matter (mater) of the material
Material has lost the matter of spirit
 ethereal.
The poles within must reverse
Life everywhere revolve, daily immerse
in the Sun, Son,
and His Love Will Be Done
or it will be the end for everyone.

34

POWERFUL POWWOW

No more do I need this drama
Done forever is this karma
I can suffer no harm
knowing always I'm held in divine arms

God is my father, my friend and lover
my son, husband and brother
Goddess is my mother, friend, beloved,
my daughter, wife, sister, grandmother

Within I must go where within I find
everything that is loving, compassionate
 and kind
Forever leave fear and loss behind
Surrender the ego and the mind

Within is love in an infinite well
where quest ends for the Holy Grail

This swirl of turmoil and inner hell
is a lie expounded by the devil

Energy extravagantly spent
in the search for enlightenment
Do not for one instant repent
for of course t'is all heaven sent

In the wilderness I did not die
In the face of persecution I did not lie
Though it seemed tears I cried would
 never dry
True feelings I did not deny

"Tis over now
I have prevailed somehow
To the divine I bow
This life is certainly a powerful powwow

35

MYSTIC AUM 11.11

Mystic marriage, mystic column
The alchemy of 11.11
Mystic love, mystic union
eleven eleven, divine communion

The arc of the covenant is by divine
decree
This is the Re-creation – divine humans
are we.
Two by to we will cross the heavenly sea
in love unions ordained celestially

The covenant through the sky will arc
as on the return voyage to heaven we
embark
The light with love will envelop the dark
This bridge to heaven will be a shining
divine landmark

Glandular magnetism drawing divine
complement
Sacred love the holy sacrament
The juices of divine love ferment
into the holy wine of heavenly intent

This is divine prophecy
The evolution of Noah's legacy
Connecting in blessed intimacy
Carried by divine communion in
vessel of the true Holy See

Embarking two's and three's in a divine
journey
across the bridge of light to gates of pillars
pearly
This path of golden rainbow light will be
walked by many
returning to harmony, a life heavenly

In rivers of light you will be raised
carrying you inexorably wave after wave
Only by divine lovelight can you be saved
Every step with love must be paved

And so it is and so it will be
Spoken from true light by divine decree
The truth of this shall be plain to see
The precession of the equinox's mystic
alchemy

The mystic column
is the celestial Aum*
we all hail from
The bridge to home

So catch those waves of this era's divine
birthright
Dance on these particles of photon light
Jump on Pegasus' back and take flight
Become one again with the Almighty

Start shining the light of the star that
you really are
For this, the truth is you are a star
Your highest essence is from afar,
waiting to be reborn since Lemuria

Now is the moment in space and time
when to divine prophecies we are to align,
foreseen by Egyptians, Hopis and Mayans,
ascension in one great, divine, tantric,
cosmic orgasm

A journey of many lives have you driven
In chariots of fire have you ridden
through spiritual deserts that lead
to heaven
This is the gateway of 11.11

if you have passed through the wilderness
Climbed mountains to eagle's nests
Journeyed the underworld night and day
without rest
Passed trials of fires burning relentless

Tossed and tumbled on stormy seas sailed
By demons and dark nights been assailed
Faced the feeling that all has failed
Then you are ready to pass
through the veils

Into a higher reality
A life of spiritual sobriety
Ecstatic in purity
Loving blissfully into eternity

Divine love is the way of Christ
The truth, the way and the light
The embodiment of the Holy Spirit
That does transfiguration illicit

It is time to know it, live it, love
and show it
And so it is and so it will be that in sacred
union we will be free spirits
So spread your angel wings and fly
to heaven
through the gateways of 11.11.

*Aum ~ Om (also spelled **Aum**) Hindu sacred
sound that is considered the greatest of all mantras,

comprising three worlds – earth, atmosphere, and heaven, three major Hindu gods – Brahma, Vishnu,

and Siva, three sacred Vedic scriptures – Rg, Yajur, and Sama. Om mystically embodies the **essence of the entire universe**. And a philosophical belief that God first created sound and the universe arose from it. A most sacred sound, Om is the root of the universe, everything that exists and continues to hold everything together.

36

WHY HIDE?

It's just light after all,
so why do we hide?
The fear of the long fall
is what we cannot abide

Do you hide from me?
What are you so afraid I might see,
that I might love thee
or I might leave?

Which would you rather?
That if you allow human love
you might lose the Father
or trust that below is as above?

Can anything be worse
that this dastardly human curse
that romantic love doeth divine love
 disperse?
Can we not this belief reverse?

What if it is true
that you are me and I am you?
Then what should we do
but make our vows anew

Time after time we come together
there is no end to this play
We have loved and will continue to
 forever
So my lover, this time please stay!

Let us not this love betray
but let it live forever and a day
Let it last until the end
together into the sun to ascend

What more could we want
than to drink from this ecstatic font
The source from which we are born
So many garbs of this love we have worn

Angels of love have healed broken wing
Trumpets with the song of swans sing

Cherubs sound their horns
as our love awakens again to a new dawn

So what will it be for you and me?
Into the devil's lair flee,
dance this love-song to the sound of the
  angel's choir
or toss away this flame into hell's fire?

On the wings of angels we could ride
Flying to heaven side by side
Knowing this love has never died
though every attempt to destroy it this
  love hath defied

For me now there can be no other way
than in this field of love to stay
Though of other emotions there is a great
  array
only love can all my fears allay

That I love you cannot be denied
though the devil may laugh at my faith
and deride

To love or not to love, you have to
 decide
Be true to love, or belie the divine, and
 hide

37

LAND OF CENTAURS
{Australia)

Lost and lonely in this land of centaurs
beating their drums, clod–hopping
 around on all fours
How I long for the wild Celt moors
abounding still with magic of unicorns

I long for the company of old souls
 living the mysteries of the old world,
Legends of the ancients being relived
 and retold,
To bathe in the lore of bards and poets
  that enfold
wrapping the soul in wings of gold

To be in Cornwall where mystery
Dances alive in every plant flower
 and tree

The magic is still there, showing itself to
  those who dare to see
Ineffable but palpable, encompassing
  fully.

These centaurs have lived a lie too long
believing power is big and strong
Insensitive to those they live among
Attuned only the sound of their own
song

They set themselves in a world void of
  empathy, apart,
void of heart
Proud and vain, they feel so smart
When what is emitted is bullshit and
  farts

Self obsessed, languishing in la–la–land
Pixies and elves burying their heads in
  the sand

Oh for a knight reaching out a feeling
  hand
who for truth, love and honour, strong
  will stand

What of the priests and priestesses of
  Avalon,
into the mists are they all gone?
In search of the elusive unicorn,
the carrier of knowledge that we are all
  one?

The land of the grail knights was pure
  and free
Merlin, Arthur, love, truth and harmony
Theirs was the true quest, the grail holy
To this they gave themselves solely

Centaurs gazing in Narcissus's pool
kicking the earth for the gold of fools
Stamping, snorting, stubborn as mules
Preaching half truths, bending the rules

Living an illusion of Elysian Fields
Feel what is real!
Wake up! Wake up! Wake up and feel!
Let your hearts open and heal!

The elements reflect crazed extremes
of illusory thought and misshapen
  dreams
All is not as it seems
There is more to oneness than puffing
  and preening

'Tis not the truth of who thou art,
what truly counts is the truly caring
  heart
That is the grail, the most holy quest
Our divine inheritance, the Celestial
  behest.

The end of the rainbow is never reached
until the walls of the heart are breached

The pot of gold that you seek
lies in the softness you think is weak.

The spirit that yields its harshness
Rides in chariot of love with divine
 harness
The heart that loves in the midst of
 starkness
The soul that shines in the hour of
 darkness

38

OH PEOPLE, HO

Oh, people of America!
How we weep for you.
Oh people of America,
the hate and anger you do not want to
acknowledge
is the hate and anger of your his-story
re-dredged
The hate that lies hidden inside
brings a world of hate alive.
The hate of your ancestors from a world
left behind
returns to haunt you unless it is owned,
signed
Your destruction of the native kind
is his-story which doeth you bind.

Oh children of Afghanistan, how we
weep for you
Oh, men and women of Afghanistan,
how we weep for you too.

What have you created?
In your repression, feminine hate,
you have brought this upon yourselves
karmic repercussions suppressing
Divine Self.

Oh, people of America, Oh, people of
Afghanistan
when will you learn to love as one?
When will you open your hearts to all,
open your souls where light of Spirit
falls,
allow the love of God and Goddess into
your spirit
to merge within it
live together in love and peace
ignite within the divine flame of ecstasy,
that bathes the entire One Universe with
Love
make below as above

Within and without
to Divine Feminine surrender all doubt

blame and shame erase
reclaim Her Love that bathes in waves
In waves of bliss of the Goddess
caress, bless, harness tenderness

Seek ever deeper within
Forgive all imagined sin

The I AM Presence resides
d e e p
within
the
I AM
of the
I AM PRESENCE
OF THE I AM
Reconnect to the inner Elohim

AHO, INSH'ALLA, AMEN,
THE PEACE HYMN

39

MERE WORDS

Mere words cannot express
human death, loss, the emptiness.

Mere words, a kind of heartlessness,
cannot console
or begin to address
the theft
of love's loving caress.

40

PARADISO INFERNO
IN THE END TIMES

Hark now my love
what was that sound
that did the earth so hard pound?

The footfall of this giant Love I have
  found
in the walls of my temple ground
Would that it would on my floor
 constantly resound
where aflame in the night I burn to be
  found
Fingers in hair to be wound
To be in your embrace entwined
Body to body thrust and grind
Divine love in humankind.

What passion therein shall we find?
Beyond all reason of human mind
just love, just pure, so refined.
Alchemical Wedding, Marriage Divine
Love's Labour Lost, rewritten, new lines
Paradiso inferno in the End Times
It's the shift of the ages
            Choose now love sublime

41

GODDESS' GOLD

As I gaze at heaven's view
my heart draws thoughts to pictures of
 you
and dandelion faeries ring me in
 gossamer hue
Away from you, every moment I rue.
Would that I knew when our
acquaintance will be renewed

I turn to the stars for the secrets they
 hold
In them the wisdom is already told
Whether you will come again with love
 so bold
and delve into my depths for my
 Goddesses' gold

Surely we must hold each other once
 more

I vision you soon, once more, at my
 temple door
On your winged horse you will return to
 my shore
igniting a love fire to light up a tor

For you have returned to me now from
 Avalon
It has been so long yet this love in my
 veins ever flows strong
The musical voice of love lives on
Memories fly by of lives bygone

We meet again
and we are still One
Your essence, unchanged, bright as the
 sun
River of divine lovelight forever runs ~

Amongst valleys and hills it finds its
 course
as the knight glides home on his horse
to the internal quest for the eternal
 stream of love, our source ~

Divine union that has no remorse
From feelings such as these there can be
no divorce
This union is truly a divine love-force

A living light of the eternal flame
Ebbs and flows, but close remains
Ever different and yet the same,
a passion no amount of lives can tame
We come back together again and again
if only to hear love's most haunting
 refrain
These waves we ride in sun, wind and
 rain
our divine heritage again to reclaim

To live a love that for a whole life lasts
To dine at the table of divine repast
Pour your nectar with love into my glass
And in the joys of such a love let us
 blissfully bask.

42

DIVINE LOVER TONIGHT
DECREE

A divine lover
by Divine right
is mine
tonight.

And so be it
And so do I decree it

43

MIRROR MIRROR

What a mirror
what a gift
what a fervour
what a love lift
Thank you, thank you, thank you, thank
you.

I know not what it is you do
but I am a cooking, juicy, sizzling stew
The mere thought of you and I'm covered
in dew

Combinations of delectable spices
the depths of magnetics in you entices
To be without this furnace is a crisis
True passion goes beyond all niceties

Living, breathing, seething fire
Love flames through veins in a glazing
quagmire

To die on this love pyre
There can be no love that takes you
 higher

Quivering, shaking, vibrating mass
yet you are gone, alas, alas!
Would that I could bind you to me with
 a sash
Lest this love die unlived in a mound
 of ash

I will let it live, I will let it breath,
I will let it ooze, enchant and seethe
I shall paint love in an exquisite love
 frieze
This rapture shall flow with ease

Mirror, mirror, on the wall
I wish for this love now, I wish for it all
To gaze into those eyes lost and
 enthralled
and wrap your seed in my favourite
 shawl

So mirror, mirror,
Come now thither
that I might kiss your shivers
Divine nectars merging in rivers

Merge in love now until the end
Cares of the mind all time transcend
To brush my hair on your feet, on knees
  I will bend
if only with you to ascend, ascend,
 ascend

44

WHEN SHALL WE TWO MEET AGAIN

Oh when shall we two meet again?
Through all dimensions, every plane
thunder, wind and rain
The timeless words of the lovers' refrain

To be or not to be
wouldst that thou be here now with me
to journey through the infinite sea
and dance in ecstatic reverie

If music be the food of love
then in your hands I am a dove
Hold my hand in velvet glove
Let us love below as we do above

Hark now who does't there go?
Is love thy friend or thine foe
It 'tis foe to you, you may go
If friend to you then let it show

Let it be
for all to see
that thee and me
and me and thee
are together, free,
free in love to be
timelessly

45

APOLLO'S GILDED TOKEN

You set me alight
You stand apart
Of you the merest sight
bursts open my heart

Your mind so bright
Your energy alert
Your rapture such height
Not a single hair on your head inert

Your knowledge so deep
Your soul divinely blessed
Even the angels must weep
with the presence you manifest

Your knowing is wondrous
Your brightness innate
Your loving tumultuous
Divine grace is your gait

Hair shining golden
Heart wide open
Your words magically spoken
Surely you carry Apollo's gilded token

46

MORNING VIEW
OF GODS & GODDESSES

My morning view
memories of You
Your touch whispering through
aura's radiant hue

Unveiling dimensions
no pretensions
Timeless suspensions
Mystery mentions

Basking in Your field
as words of truth You wield
Separateness is healed
by the softening fruit as hearts
 yield

Overflowing with life-force unbound
Universes,metaverses, You sail around
Waves lapping to Your voice's deep,
 melodic sound
Sunlight and starlight reflections found

The morning breeze kisses my cheek
as into the ethers Your lips I again seek
You swim through the astral in my rivers
 and cheeks
Cells in light bodies in ecstasy shriek

Flocks of snow white ibis flying by
as in the aftermath of love we lie
Love's dew lingering on kissing thighs
Pauses between waves of passion, sweet
 sighs

This morning view is crystal sheer
Gods and goddesses so near
New dawning in heavenly essence
  smeared
Reviewing night of love, a new day, and
  love is still here

Flaming light urging me on
giving me hope You are not gone
Glimmers of faith it will not be long
Trusting the knowing that together we
  belong

Feeling, imagining, sensing You near
Oh, my God, to me you are so dear
Do You not the cry of my heart hear?
I long to know, to know You will
  reappear

If not now, when?
Will You come to be again and again?

Though I seek You in a hundred men
You are the one for whom my heart kens

Wishing You were nearer
with me right now, right here
Our love would be a field of light,
    flowering, glistening ever sheerer,
Entire world circling with rejoicing
  cheers

47

GOOD BOLSTERING

*{A friend with a crush
on her business colleague was telling me about
his new upholstery and I replied "it sounds like
you're more into bolstering – we had a very
long laugh ~ this little tawdry ballad ensued}*

Said Belinda to Bill
"I need some good bolstering".
"I certainly will,"
replied Bill without faltering.

"I though you'd never ask,"
said he, on bended knee,
"I'm certainly up to the task.
In you I could plant many a seed."

Breathless, said she, "I've been waiting
 and waiting ~

there's a fire in me that needs placating,"
"In my wildest dreams," said he, "I've
 been anticipating.
This hunger for you I need satiating."

Swooping wildly the desk, pens and
 papers to floor
As in unison they shed clothes with
  impassioned furore
She barely had time to lock the office
 door
as they came together with a mighty roar.

PRISONERS

Prisoners of spiritual reason
purveyors of spiritual treason
Beware the pseudo–spiritual attitude
proffered with mental platitudes

True spirituality is love and care
Mind and ego stripped away, nude,
Soul laid bare

49

BRIGHT STAR

I miss you, my muse
Creation ignites when our energies fuse
I hope you're shining wherever you are,
Bright Star,
    Shine on me, lift me out of these blues

MUSES

Muses come and muses go
If one muse can be it all, I don't know
What chance of a long, lasting, beautiful
  relationship?
Who knows if in this life it will be my
  trip.

Like sparkles of diamond's many facets
More love always more love begets
This is a play of many sets
Who knows by how many we can be
  met?

The diamond does not have to be cut and
  polished to shine divine
Raw from the earth, our earth–mother's
  blood crystalline

The essence of Her heart, pure,
 unrefined.
Muses, like diamonds, are halls of
 mirrors reflecting light divine

To gaze into the mirror and see only one
would leave so many of life's songs
  unsung
Never to taste love tongue to tongue
 Or intensely gaze upon

One whom to your heart clasps strong
Yet surely, yes, one day this love will be
  done with whom you know you truly
  belong
A muse with a diamond heart, powerful,
 open and strong
So many traditions of love to chose from

A muse to amuse
A muse to peruse
A muse to bemuse
A muse with whom to fuse
A muse with whom to muse

In the end, when you have paid love's
 dues,
Each other never to lose

LOVERS' LOST LAMENT

I will let you go if you ask me,
I know I have to.
Please don't ask me.
For what you will see in my eyes
if you dare to let your gaze caress
is the pain of loves lost, unbearable
 emptiness,
and Death.

Will I die if you leave me?
Oh, no, not I,
only inside.
Will I cry if you leave me?
Tears you cannot hide,
the infinite sorrow of the lovers' demise.

When we meet again,
is it to be 'just friends,

Should we just forget
how deeply our hearts met,
Feeling would be death,
so no regrets?

Would you rather not die
than live with love's infernal lie
whose fears you cannot hide?
What is worthy inside
if you walk not with love at your
  side,
In heaven and earth, am I not your
  bride?

If all that is so
then I should be able to let you go.
Yet the core of my being screams with
  fervour,
It is here and now –
not just forever.
We came to earth for this endeavour
If not now, maybe never.

Though I let you go
I would have you know
that the flower in your heart must
 grow
The risk of hearts breaking
is love in the making.
Our love was so.

WISH YOU WERE HERE

Wish you were here
on this night so clear
Forgotten, every memory of fear,
Starlight my heart onwards steers

Moon almost full gleams
in infinite sky without seams
Ocean of my heart with effervescence
 beams
Thoughts of you dance in my dreams

Flying with the angels of the night
For so long, of you no sight,
At times no glimmer or light
Still burns yet in my heart, this love so
 bright

53

WE ARE STARS

I love you friend,
brother,
lover
All that you are,
wherever you are
Nothing this field of love can mar
We are bright stars

FLAMING SPEAR
(DIVINE AMOUR)

If your heart was pierced with a flaming
 spear
You would know how it feels to have
 You so near
Light orbiting in fiery sphere
Fills my eyes 'till my cheeks run with
 tears

What is this feeling that fills me so full
that my heart in every direction is
 pulled?
Relentless magnetism never lulls,
With wonder this feeling I can only mull

What divine connection creates such a
 draw
that you just need to bask in it more and
 more
though it leaves you sliced wide open
 and raw
Old walls of fear and pain bleeding and
 sore

This can but be divine love, I am sure
The travails were worth journeying for
Such are the blessings of eternal law
that eventually there is only this Divine
 Amour

55

FLASHES OF DESTINY

Elusive as leaves on the trees
in a season they pass you by
Flirting tauntingly, challenging the mind
which vision to time and space would
 bind

Flashes of destiny
cannot be seized
they visit awhile then take their leave
For their fulfillment never grieve

Prepare for whatever is coming with love
Messages from way up above
Destiny has its own season
Time and place are its reason

Winter spring summer or fall
if your dream still lingers unfulfilled, out
 of sight
'tis not right
 or 'tis too small

Flash of destiny
can leave you bereaved
Until one day you clearly see
that for it you are ready and worthy

So bide your time
Tend your vine
To the Divine align
and one day the sun on your day of
 destiny will shine

WINDOW OF LIBERATION

Blessed window of liberation
Most gracious salvation
Revealing a new world view
Rebirthing me anew

Lost, when this vision is removed
Found again when inner eye unglues
Do we the Self always have to lose
to find again what is really true

Spiraling round and round
lost, found, lost and again found,
We soar to the heavens
and crash to the ground

Windows come and windows go
but gradually they morph
If with diligence the seeds we sow
the window becomes a door

IN LOVE WITH LIFE

Written in Bali chez my dear friends
Don Paris and Ilona Selke
Dedicated to them with love, gratitude
and appreciation for their company
and Haven divinely sent

Falling in love with life again
a place to live, love and laugh
Little of life's struggle remains
Oh, joy of liberation and this new path

A place where Heaven and Earth dance
 in harmony
where present and past meet happily
People give smiles freely
Easy in a state of love to be

A haven for lovers to meet
Old soul friends anew to greet

Where spirits dwell within reach
and life bows down at your feet

Island of the Gods is this
Devas sway in perfect bliss,
Flowers and perfume whispering to you
 their wishes
Everything softened by Goddess's kiss

58

ONE DAY AT YOUR SIDE

*These lines were inspired by Chow Yun Fat's
immortal last words in Crouching Tiger). Words
that rip through heart and soul like a tornado
every time. I have heard and seen him speak
them many times ~ they still touch every chord
in body and soul.*

I would rather live one day at your side
than the rest of my life in heaven
Immortal words in my heart eternally
 vivified
Words to lift a heart long deadened

Love can have no greater sacrament
Human heart no deeper sentiment
Such love is heaven sent
Divine love's profound testament

Layers of non-love unpeeling
to live and love such feeling

Soul blissfully out of control, reeling
Would the Divine such a hand be
 dealing!

For one day at your side
I would pay high price
'though I would wish it for a whole life
What a destiny – to be this love's wife!

DRAGON AND PHOENIX REUNION

To run my fingers through your hair
reflecting flames of fire's embers
To gaze once more on your countenance
  so fair
The way you looked at me forever will be
  remembered

Lips long to brush your cheek
to feel you close and surrender
Love's truth in your eyes to seek
naked souls dancing undefended

Eyes deep pools of river green
gazing at me as befits a queen
Brows that crown the eyes of a king
Voice of deep velvet through entire
  being sings

To be with you my flesh burns
Thinking of you my heart turns
From feeling this will you run
or turn with me to face the sun?

Through the stars
did we fly, shining lovelight on Venus,
 Jupiter and Mars
Liquid light of love exploding with great
 sighs
Such ecstatic union was ours

Dragon reuniting with Phoenix
flying together through the sky
Kind sir, please do my feathers lick
Show me a love flame my tears to burn
 dry

Hold me in an endless kiss
Join with me in eternal bliss
Do not mislead, but lead this miss
into an eternal divine lovers' tryst

60

HANDSOME YOUNG MEN

handsome young men
beautiful faces
oh, to be young again
to be blessed by their graces

61

SCENTS AND SOUNDS
OF BALI

Flying through the night in Bali
Witch on motorbike, liberated, free
Wafting scent of sweet frangipani
burning rubbish fires, incense, cooking,
 pigs
"Hello, how are you?" from the dark of
 the trees speaks ~
Scents and sounds of Bali, bitter sweet

G'DAY MATE
{LIFE IN OZ}

G'day mate
Oh, am I late?
All in the flow
Never thought you might have
 somewhere else to go!

Now worries, mate,
only forty-five minutes wait
Oh, you have other things to do?
        – never thought of you! ~

TALK TALK TALK

Oh how people talk
They talk as they eat
They talk as they walk
They even talk in their sleep

But oh how much they miss,
the silence, the inner kiss,
the loss of gifts from angels' lips,
the wellspring of inner bliss

Silence and talk cannot co-exist
In silence hides the angels' wish
where life's jewels find sparkle,
  cut and polish
Quiet is divine love tryst

So when next you think to talk
Hush, and listen for where angels walk

In stillness you can hear their hearts beat
and blessings they whisper whilst you
 sleep

In inner stillness resides elusive
 Peace,
steps of the Masters' feet,
the softest voice of angels
and the chimes of Divine soul bells

It takes time
it takes practice
it takes love Divine
Eventually there it is
All for which you have ever pined ~
                    God's Kiss

WE ARE THE COCONUT TREES

We are like the coconut palm
Its supple fronds our etheric arms
Its fruit our abundant fertility
Sweet milk the plasma on which life's
blood feeds

Starting small
it grows so tall
to shade us from the sun
    as with earth and sky we become one

GRAPES, SWEET OR SOUR

Why are your grapes so sour?
What to you did befall
that traps your heart in vice so small
mind mean and dour?

What happened so long ago
that you still carry in your soul?
Why are you dragging around this heavy
  shadow
that runs in your soul garden like a
  mole?

What would it take for your heart to
  flower,
to let go of all that is old,
to release the lead and shine the gold
and in loving-kindness build your
  bower?

Let it go, if not now, when?
Do you want to die old and bitter,
Do you wish to relive it again and again
A life of love and joy away fritter?

Would you keep your soul locked in
 ebony tower
deprive us all of your love
or release from your heart the dove,
Soul-garden with blossoms overspilling,
 heavenly perfumed with wild flowers

66

CUSTER RE-BORN
POOR ME, POOR ME

*I had the unpleasant experience of being called
upon to work with the soul who was Custer in a
previous life.   It was emotionally and spiritually
challenging and harrowing, but enlightening.
Writing this poem was an essential catharsis
that reveals the torment of the karmic play that
cannot be repealed until all wounds are healed.
My soul of the red heart remembers, heals.*

*I dedicate this to the Indian tribes of the
Americas
who suffered more than Custer has still
to imagine
Your sacred road and souls to me feel
like Home
Hau, Mitakuyepi! Mikakuye Oyasin
Greetings, Friend! ~ To all of my relatives
AHO*

So mean-spirited
emotionally dim-witted
Split into darkness Luciferian
denial of the love Marian

Self-crucifying sabotage
black sand mirage
Like father like son
Divine Will never to be done

Mind and ego, black soul
out of control
Screaming, "I am abused,"
while twisted evil uses

Blaming and projecting unconsciously
transferring shame shamelessly
"Poor me, poor me", baby whines
"Why am I abandoned by the Divine?"

The Divine knocked so many times on
  your door
but you turned away and went back for
  more

Sacred contract for you holds no sway
hence misery you continue to perpetrate

Your own and others' suffering is your
  continued creation
"Victory!" Evil screams in elation
The light it has successfully blocked
Door to the heart banged closed and
  locked

Then again, "Poor me," it wails
"Why am I stuck in this hellish jail?
Help me, why won't you help me, please...
I'm desperate, begging on my knees"

The answer is clear and easy to find
it lives in the annals of the sadistic mind
"How dare you affront me so!
The truth I absolutely wish not to know

I'm just a victim, pure and kind
badly beaten, hard done-by, maligned
To speak thus you have no right
You are not of the light

I'm dying but I'll see you in Court
I'll sue you for your confronting thoughts
If your spiritual principles cannot be
 bought
Then by the Patriarchy you will be
 fought

To protect my ego I will fight 'till I'm
 blind
I will die to justify my righteous mind
This cancer that through me runs wild
is nothing to do with past life-denial's
 and artful guile

Why have you not yet healed it, fixed,
given your life my wounds to lick?
Instead you in falsity outrageously state
that 'tis I who does this dis-ease create

I did not want to take responsibility
I did not want this true spirituality
My past life tyranny I'm not ready or
 willing to own
nor look at how this garden I have grown

I would rather die in agony
than admit I have created this reality
But give me just a minute or two
and I will find a way to sue

That way on you I can put all the blame
and continue playing my sickly game
I demand my money back in full
so over a less astute healer's eyes I can
 pull the wool

In the meantime maybe I can hide from
 this pain
I have caused others, that returns to
  haunt me again and again
I care not how many times I cause misery
as long as you heal it and prevent it
 coming back to me

Come hell or high water I will continue
 to pretend
that the fault is all at your end
That you have beyond all bounds tried to
 help me heal I will deny
I will continue to rage and insist you lie

Though to be taken through this I
  agreed,
the light for a few days seen,
this screaming rage I do prefer
To spiritual ignorance and karmic denial
  I continue to err

A healer of a different kind I will find,
one who will be my walking stick as I go
  blind
As long as they support my ruse
to scream "Abused!" at truth whilst I
  abuse

Poor me, poor me, how can you be so
  bold
to show me the darkness in mine soul
That is not how I want to heal
I want to kick, blame and squeal

I have paid you and now I own you
you must do what I want you to
I have not paid you for your expertise
I have paid you to collude with me

I care not for sacred contract
with lawyers (like my father) I will
 attack, fight back
though of course I am nothing like he
He and my mother were so mean to me

Poor me, Poor me
I am not them, nor they me
I really have no time to die
I'm too busy to myself lying

This cancer is not my disease
It really has nothing to me to teach
I prefer my ego to justify
my version, my 'story' forever to keep
 alive

No matter about past or future lives
and how the true story will continue to
 thrive
alcohol, drugs, chemo then morphine
These are not my lungs, liver or spleen!

Speak not to me of the Divine
For it I have no time

I prefer lawyer's rites and to be right
than accept Divine truth and light

Poor me, poor me, poor me, poor me!
Why am I suffering ongoingly,
How many years and lives will this go
   on?"
"As long as you continue to sing the
   same song!

You see, there is nothing out there, only
   you
There is none to blame, no one to sue,
Only through forgiveness and making
   amends
can Custer his brutal past transcend

Forgive everyone, everything and self
Into the darkness of your own soul delve
Damnation or salvation, the choice is
   yours
through re-incarnation's infinite doors

Choose now and choose wisely
You are creating your reality

You want your future to shine bright
or in suffering and continued pain be
 right?"

Poor me, poor me, poor me, poor me,
or blessed be, blessed be, blessed be,
It is up to you to chose – the choice is
 free
Choose wisely, you cannot prevail over
 Divine Reality

I REST MY CASE

You asked about the darkness of your
 soul
Well there it is, clear and bold
There is nothing on your human legal
 floor
that comes close to karmic law
Exactly this is the cause of your fate
Choose love or choose hate
Game over, check mate!
I rest my case

LAUGHED OUT OF COURT

(Custer dialogue contd.)

Laughed out of court ∼
in truth t'would be naught
Laughed out of heaven ∼
that would be the worst Armageddon
  Up to you, General, you choose!

69

ON YOUR KNEES

(Custer dialogue contd.)

When you bow down on your knees
cry, "I'm ready to surrender,
let me in, please,"
then suffering will be ended
From pain you will be reprieved,
the rift in your soul mended
But one thing you must believe,
you will be arduously tried and tested
By ego be not deceived
You must remain on your knees utterly
 undefended
There exists no other way to be relieved
of the ways your soul hath offended
Of might or right you are fully bereaved
 'til To True Caesar, what is truly His,
  must be rendered

You can only enter Heaven on knees
 bended
Of God you cannot take your leave
Love of God must be tended

When life no longer can breathe
all roads endangered
To deny God is to remain a thief
meanness bitterly vented
to wallow indefinitely in grief
Soul ne'er to be attended
'tis time to turn back both cheeks
with God again be befriended

Before the dawn
the darkest hour
all light is gone
all sense of power
But, little soul, be not scared,
light will again the day shower
when heart and soul have been bared
given up the ivory tower
God's love and understanding will be
 shared
and new life again will flower

70

HEAVEN'S GATE

Of death, dear one, be not afraid
eternal life in Heaven is made
How you lived life and what you gave
determines your fate,
were you weak or were you brave,
how many lives did you help to save,
how much of your heart you gave.
Did you brighten other people's days
or spend your time tending your grave?
How many spirits did you raise,
or in self-pity did you laze?
Did you bully and threaten to get your
   way,
or in your garden let angels play?
At the Divine were you continually
   amazed,
or by the Devil were you soothsaid?
Did you turn, God/Goddess to face,
or did you turn away?

All this determines how much grace
shines in your soul space
The end of life is just a phase
soul cannot be dis-created, erased
but one day your soul you will have to
 face
Actions you cannot obliterate
False ego must be irradiated
To God/Goddess your spirit raised
So, be brave, your soul embrace
"tis only you who determines your fate
God/Goddess is love, not man-made
Of yourself, not They, be afraid
At Heaven's Gate, love awaits

71

BRIDE OF CHRIST

Passion strikes with blinding light
Wielding force of great might
Eyes open wide, blinding sight
When everything feels just right.

What to do
when it shines on you?
Where to go
when you love someone so?

Eyes of blue,
startling hue,
Shining so bright on you
you can't see through.

What if you saw?
What if you showed up?
Can there be anything more
once you've drink from love's cup?

What would be revealed,
a heart unhealed?
Lost in a field
of feelings unsealed?

Where to go
when caught in love's throes?
What to do
when there's only you?

Hide from the smile
that does't so beguile?
Shield the heart
from the love thou art?

When you lie in the arms
that surround you in calm
Spirit resteth in shade of palm
and soul's softened with velvet balm.

When love shines its blinding light
on you
There's nothing at all that you
can really do.

Will there ever be another you
or this heart be forever blue?

What is the force
that steers love's course?
Where does it go?
Can we ever know?

Am I now lost,
to four winds tossed?
As elusive autumn leaves I am scattered
on the breeze.
Without you, bereaved.

What to do
when love shines its infinite light
on you?
Of love's infinite cup I imbued
when into my dreams you flew.

Hope comes and goes
with the highs and the lows.
Do I choose enlightenment
and let go of excitement?

This love doeth heal my heart's rent.
Were you not heaven sent?
When the beat of my heart slows
I hear Pan's flute softly blow.

Tell me, amour,
when I again knock on your door
will you hide from me your core,
turn your back on all promise of
love's lore?

If we are forever apart
how will I close the door to my heart?
A whole meadow of flowering
pink yarrow
could not heal this wound of
Cupid's arrow!

Stranded on a reef,
coral the color of unspoken grief!
Night, the full moon shineth,
of peace it is my thief.

Memories of you flow
with each star glow.

Beyond space and time
will destiny again make you mine?

When passion shines its blinding light
on you
to all reason we say adieu.
What to do
with this love for you?

So fare thee well my friend
'till we meet again.
Be it this life before the end,
the next, or when we ascend.

In the field of dreams
or some far-flung shore
will you float in with the sunbeams
or knock on my door?

For what can I do
when I see you anew,
but heart be true
and drink from your dew?

What to do when passion burns
inside of you,
searing heart with amber hue?
Lovelight without which we cannot do
Can I learn to live without you?

Will we dance forever to this endless
love's song?
What restless dreams will I
find you among?
Or to this moment only does it belong?
Does each moment apart have to
take so long?

How will I find you again at the end
of this life,
questing through eons, searching
and strife?
Will fulfilled love again make
me its wife?
Is this divine love, to be bride of Christ?

72

DIVINE LIFE

Feeling the peace
Life taking on new lease
Struggle ceasing
trauma releasing
The long hard road
is reaching its goal
Relentless pace slowed
future of gold unfolds
Divine Lord is coming back in
Together the divine plan we will begin
A different way of living
teaching the way of love and forgiving
The temples I will now build
with great masters to be filled
Creating together a new world
of wisdom and sacred pearls
a world of enlightenment
blessed by hold sacrament
divine life finally manifests
a new paradigm divinely blessed

73

SAIL LOVE HOME

Swaying trees
sea breeze
dancing leaves
Why are you not here with me?

My spirit the candle-flame
flickering with amber light
If you will be here with me again
this flame will burn stronger through the
 night

Are you really coming back to me?
Absence's waves are long and lonely
Like the horizon of the infinite blue sea
our two ships in this ocean of separation
 will again meet

Clouds that move across the sky
of shapes and forms, dissolve like
 memories

flow toward me and never run dry
of this love of ours that will never cease

In my dreams home to me you will come
as surely as dawn rises to meet morning
 sun
On white horses to my shore you will
 run
and my tree will again burst with
 fragrant blossom

So my love, do not tarry long
ere my summer fruit be gone
A season like this is once n a lifetime
A harvest fit for a King Divine

We can dance like the jacaranda trees
flowering blossoms floating on the
 breeze,
swim with the lotus petals in the sea
and sail love home to eternity

74

DIVINE LOVE'S
SACRED CONTRACT

A man who's waited three quarters of his
 life
for his beloved,
the woman who would be his divine wife
Divine love finally uncovered
A sacred contract
made with the Divine
More than fifty-five years to enact
before I could be thine
This love's judgement day looms
We two will star in our own divine play
"ere the rise of the next full moon
"You are the One" we will say
And when this incredible love
 comes to light
There will be nothing to do
but stay forever in each others' sight
wordlessly communicating "I love you"

When these eyes in love meet
long lost souls again greeting
destiny will be complete
There will be nothing like these hearts
  beating
A love that never ends,
lovers, partners, best friends,
that for eons apart makes amends
A love that all other loves transcends
So, beloved, come to me soon
Linger not long on the horizon where
  you loom
Let time and space no longer our love
  doom

Come to me for the next full moon
Dance with me under the stars
Let the night not tear us apart
feelling, breathing, heart to heart
This love long awaited must finally be
  ours!

75

HOW WONDERFUL LIFE IS
THAT YOU'RE
IN THIS WORLD

Silver pearls scattered on water
sparkling mirror bejeweled
Clouds across moonlit sky saunter
glowing orb of moon around cloud's edge
 beveled

Stars hide from full moon light
Flying fish soar to greet her
Phosphorescence sets deep water alight
Moonlit air is softer, sweeter

Moon in fullness rises in every birth-
 place
Each lunar cycle a new face
filling the world with the Mother's Grace
whose marvel of magic unfailingly doeth
 Soul amaze

Gentle lulling of the waves
rolling across water's silver rays
From new beginnings to full bloom
our souls dance to Mother Moon's tune

Though She spirals around
through cycles of time and space
with infinite creation She abounds
Her seasons feelings displace

Dancing with the ocean tide
filling and emptying emotions to her
 design
These moonbeams we must learn to ride
painting life's canvas with out own
 design divine

Indigo night's silver sea
depends upon Mother's necklace of moon
 beams
We need Her to light up our dreams
to remind us we are magic, infinitely

76

LIGHT OF GREAT MYSTERY

A love light on the horizon
Little boats float on wide open ocean
The inner light guides our journey
lighthouse to fishing boat far out to sea

Distant horizon meets the sky
like human frontier meeting Divine
Love, the light of the soul,
showing the only way home

Until behind the horizon hiding
births the full moon rising
then life's sea gently illumined with silver
 rays
Sparkles on the water like filigree lace

Human life's brightest hours
As Divine waves hello to us from stars

sparkling in indigo night sky, reminding
 us we are at one
Then Sun will rise as Moon has done

Life will ever amble along
Seen or unseen Divine always smiles
 upon
however hard it may be
Great Spirit always is there with you on
 that wide open sea

So steer your vessel away from wind's lee
Raise your sails to be filled with
 breeze
Set your sights on the inner horizon,
 trustingly,
 and sail away into Great Mystery

77

One Day

One day I'll sail back into the world
wings unfurled
The spear that into my heart was hurled
that left my heart bleeding and cold,
spun my soul in a dangerous whirl
My sails soaring, velvety white
will be lifted on eddies of divine light

One day I will soar to great heights
God in full sight
to be held in the arms of an angel,
 so tight,
to touch the face of an angel and fill
 with starlight

One day I'll dance in the arms of a
    Wizard
eyes joined in starshine, loving and
 beloved

Wings encircling, held in cocooning nest,
peacefully nuzzling chest
Dancing through veils infinitely blessed
the world we will make our heavenly
 place
Divine grace
Flowering hearts of the human race
infesting dreams of visions we have
 chased
Woven stories of filigree lace
of times gone by
when we could not fly
and we cried tears that never ran dry.
Remembering our wings we'll smile as
 we cry
tears of joy as close together we lie

One day I'll touch again the face of an
 angel
merging in dancing light ethereal
It will stay, loving the feel
of the kissing of hearts that know only
 love is real
Isis and Osiris reunited in vessel celestial

One day Isis will return
in the bow of her vessel, Osiris astern
They will dance on a bed of ferns
Around them, soaring swans, ibis and
 tern
the flame of love in them so strongly
 burns

One day we will all spread our wings
and soar in the heavens where celestial
 choir sings
Bells from church spires everywhere ring
From Muslim towers a new chant singing
Church spires ringing a new dawn's
 hymns
Unfurled,
Swirled
 in heavenly meanderings.

POSTSCRIPT

AUTHOR'S BLESSING

May you ever find
The light divine
That behind shadows shines.
Remember, 'tis always thine.

ABOUT THE AUTHOR

Rev. Dr. Swan A. Montague is a mystic, visionary, artist, writer and poet, with an M.A in spiritual Philosophy and a Ph.D. in metaphysics. She is a medical intuitive and an experienced practitioner in sacred art and healing. She also creates the stunning sacred wall hangings known as Temple Veils from antique eastern silks, jewels and crystals.

Swan has lived and taught advanced metaphysics and mastery of the healing arts throughout Europe, the U.S., Australia and Mexico.

12 years ago Swan was given 3 months to live. She went into seclusion to heal herself and be in divine communion with Jesus and other divine masters. She had many close encounters with death and after one such near passing Jesus appeared and guided her back through time. Thereafter in revelatory bursts of light, memory and feeling, she wrote *"The Book of Sahra, Jesus' Secret Wife"* under her pen name, Sahra Renata.

Rev. Dr. Swan Montague is author of the quartet, *The Book of Sahra, Jesus' Secret Wife,* Book I, {*Golden Roses' Sacrifice*} is available now on Amazon.

Dr. Swan is also featured in Celeste Yacoboni's *How do you Pray?* with Gregg Braden, Marianne Williamson, Matthew Fox, Father Bede Griffiths, Byron Katie, Andrew Harvey, Dan Millman, Mirabai Starr, and more...

Swan is also co-author in *The Spirit of Abundance,* with Sandy Forster, Brian Tracy, Mark Victor Hansen & Jack Canfield (*Chicken Soup for the Soul* & The Secret), Arielle Ford (New York Times bestselling author, publicist for Wayne Dyer, Deepak Chopra and many others)

COMING SOON:

"Gold for the Soul"

More about Swan's writing
and divine sacred art
(Temple Veils)
can be found at:

www.DrSwanMontague.com

FB:
https://www.facebook.com/Swan
aka SahraRenata

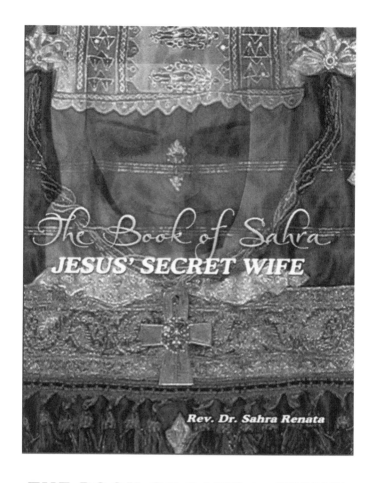

The Book of Sahra
JESUS' SECRET WIFE
Rev. Dr. Sahra Renata

THE BOOK OF SAHRA, JESUS' SECRET WIFE

Every few years, a book comes along that could change our world forever...

Sahra's story is a powerful, illuminating and deeply moving portrayal of Jesus' intimate life with His secret wife, and is the journey of all humans' remembering our divine origins. It is an authentically sacred and profound expose of their love life, an exotic, poetic romance in the light of totally new and unique understanding of the holy journey that is both beautifully sensual and sacred.

This lyrical work of art and creative inspiration gives the reader a vividly evocative experience of their way of life. Illustrated with unique sacred art exquisitely crafted from antique eastern silks, the book takes the reader on an astonishingly beautiful journey into the realm of the Divine.

A heart-wrenching tale of love and sacrifice, crucifixion and resurrection, *The Book of Sahra* uncovers essential truths about our world, our destiny, and our own innate connection to the Divine. Everyone will want to read this book and discover the deeper meaning of events 2000 years ago that made Jesus the most venerated healer/teacher ever and their relevance to humanity and the world today. In the vein of such transformational works as *The Alchemist, The Shack,* and *Conversations with*

God, this is a book for all who long for the eternal experience of Divine Love.

"Sahra's art is the highest spiritual art on the planet today. This is not just sacred art – these are divine emanations." Andrew Harvey, mystic, Rumi scholar, teacher

"Beautiful, absolutely beautiful, I didn't want to put it down and cried all the way through" Dominique Vollaers, Oracle

"This book is the literary equivalent of fine art, absolutely amazing, poetry in motion— a literary work of art of the highest order" Simon Whittaker, Healer

"I found the book utterly inspiring, so much so I read it three times, in one night. It just spoke to my heart. The prose was exquisite, and I found it poetically, very romantic, and so original in its concept. That Dr. Renata envisioned this information of Sara Jesus's secret wife before the Papyrus was discovered & later authenticated just adds to my belief that this divine work of art was obviously written from the soul of Sara Renata. A truly inspirational & a heart wrenching exquisite work of art" S. Brecknell

"This is one of the most powerful books I have ever read and one of the greatest stories of love, Sahra and Jesus love easily brings me into the euphoria of that Divine. I was anxious to read on but didn't want the story to end." Bruce Becvar, musician, composer

Order your copy of
The Book of Sahra, Jesus' Secret Wife
now on Amazon

http://www.amazon.com/Caviar-Soul-general/dp/1494489783/ref=sr_1_sc_1?ie=UTF8&qid=1387253957&sr=8-1-spell&keywords=Cavira+for+the+Soul

Made in the USA
Charleston, SC
20 April 2015